Coming to My Last Days (on the Planet)

Kent Philpott

EVP
Earthen Vessel Publishing

Coming to My Last Days (on the Planet)

©2024 by Kent Philpott

All rights reserved.
Earthen Vessel Media, LLC
San Rafael, CA 94903
www.earthenvesselmedia.com.com

ISBN: 978-1-946794-42-0
Interior design by KLC Philpott

Any part of this publication may be reproduced, stored in a retrieval system, or transmitted in any form or by any means, electronic or mechanical, including photocopying, recording, or by any information retrieval system, without the written permission of the author or publisher.

Contents

Introduction	5
1: Is My Memory Slipping?	7
2: Getting Rid of Stuff	9
3: Making Out a Will	11
4: Someone My Age Shouldn't Be Coaching Sports	12
5: Is My Father Looking Back in the Mirror?	14
6: Burial or Cremation? and Where?	16
7: Talk to Someone about Your Feelings and Fears	18
8: Seek Healing of Broken or Damaged Relationships	19
9: Spend More Time in Prayer and Bible Study	21
10: Keep Moving	23
11: Call Family and Friends Often	25
12: What about Our Past Sins?	27
13: Show Up Often at Your Local Church	30
14: Read, Read, Read	33
15: See Your Doctor and Take Your Meds	34
16: Follow Sports Teams	36
17: Last Days on the Planet	38
18: Look to Jesus	39
Other Titles	40

Introduction

I recently turned 82, and despite my feelings, I decided to talk about what is going through my heart and mind at this point in my life.

Yes, I am going to face up to this period of my life, my last years. No idea how many are left for me—one, five, a dozen, or perhaps only a few weeks—though I feel perfectly fine right now.

My dad died at age 90, his death due to some rotten sausage that got lodged in his gut, but I could see his decline years before that. My mother died, badly, at age 75; one of my brothers died of a horrible cancer when he was 74; and my youngest brother committed suicide a year after returning from Vietnam. He was a combat engineer with the Army and went through terrible times.

And let me make it clear that, though I am a Bible-believing Christian, I do not believe, and not even close, that my death date is determined ahead of time by the Creator.

The reason for my writing this booklet is to let readers know that we all, mostly, have or will experience what I am undergoing right now, and that is coming face to face with the fact of dying some time or another, maybe sooner rather than later. It is better to face it, admit the anxiety surrounding this reality, and process it for both our emotional and spiritual well-being—as well as that of others among family and friends.

This is a 'little book,' inexpensive to buy and a quick read, something to give to others.

1:
Is My Memory Slipping?

Just yesterday, while talking with an old friend about how the 49ers lost to the Kansas City Chiefs in the Super Bowl, I could not remember Brock Purdy's name, couldn't get it out of my mouth.

Since Brock is the young Niner's quarterback, I must have said his name dozens of times before during this season. For a moment I was frozen, but then I managed to say his last name, and my friend said, "Yeah, Brock Purdy," like he could see I was somehow unable to get the name out.

I have been thinking about this event ever since, with a hint of fear in me, that my lapse was evidence of mental decline. Frankly, I am not sure of this, but it is far from the first time such has happened with my beady little brain.

Is it possible that, due to my age, there is too much stored up in my bean that causes such lapses? I doubt that, but what is going on?

Now that I am working on this lead chapter, I am having to admit that this is happening to me more often that I would like. I mean, this is happening to me a lot. And, I wonder (and fear), will it get worse?

Well, what if it does? No, really I should say, "So what if it does!" No harm has been done due to my memory difficulty, of course, but still there is within me the evidence that I am getting older and that there are going to be changes in me, both physically and mentally as I age.

Maybe there are exercises I could do, medicines to take, and so on, but I am just going to have to accept the fact that I am naturally losing some of my faculties. And it just occurred to me that others can detect what is going on inside of me. It could get embarrassing. Wish it were not so, but that aspect of my experience is certainly common and is part of what prompted writing this booklet for others to know they are not alone.

I guess I am no longer the brightest bulb on the tree.

2:
Getting Rid of Stuff

My fishing poles, about a dozen of them, with lots of other stuff, are already gone.

I happened to be in a Big Five store a few months ago, and I ran into several of the varsity football players from the local high school where I joined the football coaching staff last year, mostly as the "old encouragement coach." They were looking at fishing poles. I already had it in my mind to get rid of mine, and I told the guys I would get my collection to them, and this happened at the "awards banquet" at the end of the season.

My dad taught us Philpott boys how to fish when we were little kids, and we fished in the Willamette and Columbia rivers when living in Portland, Oregon, and I admit it hurt me some to give my all equipment away.

Now I am wondering what to do with all my baseball stuff. For eighteen years, I coached the baseball team at San Quentin Prison, which is a ten-minute ride from where Katie and I live, and there are bags of uniforms given to us by the San Francisco Giants and the Oakland A's, plus caps, batting helmets, a few mitts, and maybe a dozen or so pairs of cleats. My collection fills up a shed in the back yard. This stuff has to go, and I want it in younger hands that will appreciate it.

Then I have collections of old magazines, vinyl records, sheet music, and baseball cards, some by the hundreds. My plan, decades ago, was that I would acquire the stuff and sell it when I retired. But of course, I never retired and never will, so this stuff has to go.

And tools of all sorts, including two types of saws that are yet in boxes never opened. My plan is to invite over some of the guys in the church I pastor and give most of them to those who can still make good use, even an income with them. Maybe there are a few tools I may yet need.

The above is just some of the "stuff" taking up space around the house, and I am thinking of putting a notice on "Next Door" for neighbors to come over on a Saturday afternoon to take what they want. Better than loading it up and going to the dump. Yeah there will be some regrets after doing this, but I sure don't want someone else to have to deal with it all.

3: Making Out a Will

This is a must, for the sake of family and friends. What chaos can result when a will is not carefully prepared!

And it needs to be done professionally, or at least, the final version should at least be notarized, and many copies made and then distributed to those named in the will.

Currently, my brother's family is caught up in a legal mess. He died a slow and painful death, and toward the end, he was not thinking clearly. He had made out a will in which I was to receive a fairly large amount of money, and his son was to inherit a very nice apartment house. I had read the will.

However, a family member tore that will up and created another one, deliberately leaving me and my brother's son completely out. Presently, the issue is in court, and this is one of the reasons for my putting in this piece.

Confession time now: I have not completed my will. It needs a little work, then it will be notarized, and copies distributed. I owe this to my family and so do you.

There now, I got a little tough.

4:
Someone My Age Shouldn't Be Coaching Highschool Sports

This is not completely true, as I will be coaching JV football again in the Fall, but from what our head varsity baseball coach seems to think, at 82, I am too old. And this hurts. And the regular season begins next week, February 26, 2024.

This would have been my 21st year coaching high school baseball, some years each at Tamalpais, Novato, and Terra Linda high schools in Marin County. And yeah, I supposed I could look around and call the athletic directors at a few schools, but I have decided to let it go.

My baseball coaching career started at age 15—Little League—in a suburb of Los Angeles called Sunland-Tujunga. Then I coached while in the military—a team made up of medics at Travis AFB in Fairfield, CA—and then eighteen years coaching the baseball team at San Quentin Prison. We were the San Quentin Giants, since the San Francisco Giants major league team gave us lots of uniforms and other gear. I also started an 8-man flag football team at the prison, called The Blues Brothers.

While at San Quentin, I wrote three books on the baseball program there, Season 2010, 2011, and 2012. The 2010 book, called *Strike Three, You're Out!* has 107 photos in it and is available at Amazon.com. Yes, I'm plugging my own book, but lots of folks love it.

American football is a very complicated game, known as the third most complex sport of them all, with only boxing and ice hockey numbers one and two. Last year, I was supposed to be the special teams coordinator, but I failed, was replaced, and now function as just what I call an "encouragement coach." Since I love encouraging the kids, that is just fine with me now, and they all gather around me to talk, which they don't do with the other very busy team coaches.

Some years back, while coaching the junior varsity baseball team, with a game at our school, Tamalpais High in Mill Valley, the visiting team rolled out an older man in a wheelchair, around the fourth inning, into the space for the first base coach. The home plate ump raised his hands, jumped out, and yelled to get the wheelchair off of the infield. I was about 70 then, and I wanted to charge the ump, whom I knew, and insist it was okay.

I didn't do anything, for in a second or two I knew the ump was right. I mean, could this guy get out of the way of a line drive? Likely not, but I felt bad about it and walked from the third base dugout, across the field, and spoke some soothing words to the white-haired guy in the chair, and then thanked the guy who rolled him out for his effort.

Something like this all just happened—my not being wanted because of my age, and frankly, I have not recovered from the loss. Part of my recovery process is writing this piece.

5:
Is My Father Looking Back at Me from the Rearview Mirror?

No, it wasn't my father. It was me I saw when I glanced up at the rear-view mirror while driving my car. Wow! Have I ever aged, and it is plain for all the world to see.

Here is just another thing that impacts us, and we will have to admit the reality of it. Am I right in thinking this experience might be more troublesome for women than it is for men?

Just yesterday afternoon, while at Marin TV in San Rafael, where we film our television programs (see them at milleravenuechurch.org and multiple streaming platforms), there was this closeup of me on a screen that I could see, since we were zooming our interview with a brother in Prescott, Arizona. Oh my! All the wrinkles, facial sags, and a hair line that has been steadily receding were right there for all the world to see, but most impacting, for me to see.

There is nothing I can do about it, since I am not the type to get a face lift or anything similar. It's hard for me to write this, but it is truth itself. Here I am, not that I ever thought I was handsome or good-looking. Long ago, when I was fourteen years old, I overheard my aunt Cleo say, "Oh Kent, he is kind of homely." I didn't know what the word homely meant, but I found out the next day in a dictionary at the school's library. Homely, okay, I can deal with it, but how I look now...

Acceptance is where I have to go. I am thinking of a lady now in our congregation, as old or older than I am, and I doubt people think that she is sort of ugly and old looking. But she has a wonderful smile, and that changes everything. Me? Not much of a smiler, but as I am writing this, I think I will step it up. And when I look up at the rearview mirror, or any other mirror, I will give myself a smile.

6:
Burial or Cremation? and Where?

Like you, dear reader, I would rather not have to deal with this issue. But better now than later or never, especially if no plans are made and it suddenly falls into the lap of a family member or friend. So, let's face it.

Regarding the burial or cremation question, burial is way more expensive these days, and way more complicated for those who have to arrange things.

When I visit Los Angeles, where my brother, mother, and grandmother are buried, I sometimes drive out there and see if I can remember the locations of the graves. This it is emotionally painful for me, and frankly, I have not done this now for at least ten years.

My dad's and other brother's ashes are in my office here at home. Early on, I looked at these little vases and thought of them, then glanced up and looked at a few old photos with all of us Philpotts in them. Mostly the sadness has gone away but not entirely. Recovery from the deaths of loved ones may take us many years and may never disappear altogether.

During the course of my ministry, I have officiated at around 300 funerals, including both burials and cremations. And these are important to arrange, both emotionally, physically, and spiritually. We have to be able to say goodbye, face the reality of the loss, and deal with what is often the unfinished business remaining between us and the deceased. Yes, sometimes multiple events may have occurred that were never thoroughly dealt with, and the emotional debris can linger for years. But it is better to face these matters early on, because they will not go away without sincere and deliberate processing.

I suddenly recall an incident that happened decades ago, and it has to do with whether or not it is biblical to cremate. The idea was that for resurrection to occur, there had to be a body, so no cremation. This notion is biblical err. The moment a Christian dies, he or she is present in heaven with our Lord. Besides, what about many sincere Christians who died in a fire or even a burning at the stake? A distant relative of mine, Sir John Philpott, died that way in 1555 during the reign of Queen Mary in England. He died for his faith, and I am completely confident he has been with Jesus in heaven ever since!

I have already made up my mind: I am going with cremation. And I know where, too, at a memorial park nearby. And I will request that my ashes will be in about seven little vases and then distributed to family members.

Some of us will actually look forward to leaving the planet. The older we get, with the attendant disabilities, aches, and pains showing up, it is acceptable to say to death, "I'm ready, let's do it." I have been at the bedside of some who just stopped the medications and said, "Enough is enough." Nothing wrong here.

Finally, something about the fear of dying that we all will experience to one degree or another. And this is whether one is a Bible-believing Christian or not. Yes, even though I will be with Jesus the moment after I'm dead, it is perfectly normal to not want to die and to be filled with fear and anxiety as we see our death approaching. Medical science has devised many ways to lessen these fears, and it is perfectly acceptable to avail ourselves of them.

7:
Talk to Someone about Your Feelings and Fears

My background was in psychology: two college degrees and ten years, throughout the 1970s, of operating what I called The Marin Christian Counseling Center, located in our Christian bookstore on the Miracle Mile in San Rafael, California. Tuesday through Friday I counseled, usually about six appointments a day, and I never charged a cent. Yes, some would slip me some bucks.

As a pastor, I am still counseling—not at the center, but now mostly over the phone, either calling or even texting, and in person on Saturday and Sunday mornings when I am present at the building that houses our Miller Avenue Church in Mill Valley, California. This is my fortieth year as pastor.

My point is, it is vitally important that we have someone to talk to—someone who will listen, will not direct or order, but listen and listen and not reveal anything that was said to them. I have one of these, my wonderful wife Katie. In addition, I have an old friend from high school days and also an old friend who actually is a professional counselor who conducts his work over the phone, and he counsels me for free. I've got it made!

We all have to have someone to talk to, a person whom we trust, and who will listen, maybe make a comment or two, but who actually, truly listens! Make this connection, even if you have to pay for it.

Hope you are listening.

8:
Seek Healing of Broken or Damaged Relationships

Maybe broken, maybe damaged, maybe even worse, but I've seen how negative events may still have impact many years later.

There is little chance for a person to live numbers of decades and not be either offended and hurt or offend and hurt someone else. This is life.

Right now, I total up at least six of these, and four can never be healed, because the person I either offended of who offended me is no longer on the planet. There it is, so it is time for me to act with the other two.

If I have been hurt in some manner, what can I do? My sense is that I really don't want to bring up an incident, since it might cause even more distress; in fact, it might come over as an accusation and then make things even worse. Okay, I am going to forget about it, which I think will help relieve much of my trauma.

If I have brought pain, suffering, and/or sorrow to another person—a family member, friend, neighbor, wife, son, daughter—what can be done? Well, some kind of communication is in order, maybe person to person, or a letter, a phone call, maybe a text message, but some means of communication to ask for forgiveness. The person on the other end may disregard it, become even more upset, or it could bring some healing either sooner or later. As I am writing this, I'm thinking of two such situations that resulted in some damage that I would love to be freed from.

The above has to do with real life incidents here in real time, but there is another dimension, and this is accepting forgiveness from our Lord and forgiving ourselves. This latter part of the sentence does not mean forgiving ourselves as if it were blotted out of our conscience, but acceptance of hurting others in some fashion and realizing the truth of it. We were careless or even cruel, and our actions or words did definitely cause pain and suffering.

We can seek forgiveness and be content with at least that much. But we cannot expect to control the thoughts and emotions of others.

A passage of Scripture just came to mind: "If we say we have no sin, we deceive ourselves, and the truth is not in us. If we confess our sins, he is faithful and just to forgive us our sins and to cleanse us from all unrighteousness." 1 John 1:8–9 (ESV)

There it is. For me, it means that at least, though I have hurt others, and I know I have, either willingly or unwillingly, upon my confession I receive complete forgiveness, and this is what counts the most.

9:
Spend More Time in Prayer and Bible Study

I am assuming that those of us who are retired may have more time on our hands than previously. And this can trouble us. I know this because it has begun happening to me.

Not that I have slowed down that much, but I am not coaching high school baseball now for the first time in over twenty-one years. It has a strange impact on me, and it can make me feel downcast. Normally, I would be heading to the field about 3:30 pm, but now that time is empty space.

This can be turned around, however. One way for us as Christians is to spend good time reading the Word and praying. What worked for me was to read three chapters in the Old Testament, starting with Genesis, then three Psalms, a chapter of Proverbs, then three chapters in the New Testament. And this not a rapid read, but slowly, thoughtfully, and reflecting on each chapter.

Then some prayer time. I recommend creating pages something like what is below.

Date * Subject of the Prayer * Any Answer * Date of Answer

Over the course of time, you may have many pages so designed and many answers. I found that some, even many of the prayers, did not have an answer. And in these cases, it was good for me to look at the prayers that were not answered, sometimes prompting me to look into issues if I could.

If need be, get a Bible with large font, and I recommend the English Standard Version (ESV), as it is easier to grasp the content than with some others. It is a word-for-word translation in current English, but other versions are available that translate thought-for-thought, such as the New International Version (NIV).

Being a follower of Jesus means spending time in fellowship with Him, by means of praying and reading the Scripture. I have witnessed over my pastoral ministry, that folks who did this found it to be both very enlightening and comforting.

10:
Keep Moving

That's right, keep moving, even if it hurts. Sure, the pain shoots down your back, and your sore knees and hips feel like they need to be replaced, and your shoulders ache. Your doctor may write out a prescription to ease some of these unpleasant pains, yet the need is still to keep moving!

I started going to the gym when I was 39 years old, and I have not stopped since. Currently, Katie and I go to the Jewish Community Center just a mile-and-a-half drive (or walk) down the road from us. Katie has considerable pain in her hips and legs, and so we take the elevator up to the primary floor where the workout area is. I am not as strong as during my peak years—25 pounds lighter and no longer able to bench press 225 pounds. But I work out as much as a I can, pushing my heartbeat into the 120s on the bike and the tread mill three times a week.

All these benefits, plus we have made friends with many on staff and with other members, and we look forward to it always. It is no small thing, mixing with others, young and old, in pursuit of physical fitness, since social fitness comes along for the ride.

Then the walks. We live close to the waters that enter from the Pacific, coming in from under the Golden Gate Bridge and drifting north in the Bay extending up toward Sacramento. In our neighborhood, it creates an inlet that comes about two blocks away from us, and we walk the levees about once a week, a mile long trek.

We live in Santa Venetia, a suburb of San Rafael, two miles east of the Marin County Civic Center, designed by Frank Lloyd Wright in the early 1960s. Our house is a small three-bedroom, two-bath house, nothing grand at all, but we have a great back yard that stretches up against a hill, and we plant everywhere. As I write this, Katie is headed to Home Depot to get more plants to plant. I want some peppers, I told her—green, yellow, and red. It keeps us busy; it keeps us moving, and this so precious to us.

11:
Call Family and Friends Often

At least three decades ago, I started making a list that now contains about forty names. I love sitting out in the backyard in the afternoons, especially when the sun is out, talking to family members and friends. About half of the forty are people who are part of Miller Avenue Church, so this could also be called pastoral care.

Most often, these are not long conversations, but some require settling into the stream of exchange. It is so good to call folks I used to do ministry with fifty years ago, and family members are a priority—my five kids, cousins, a former wife—plus buddies I went to high school with. Though I don't keep track, it is my idea and my desire to talk with most everyone about once every two weeks, and about one-fourth of the time, I receive rather than make the call.

Politics is not something I address in these calls. Even the folks who attend our dinky Miller Avenue Church do not know how I vote nor how Katie votes. We talk sports, baseball, and football mostly, and sometimes the conversations get spiritual. Mostly, we talk about what we are doing, about the old days, about others we all know and love. We talk about our kids, grandkids, and probably too much about our aches and pains.

And most poignantly, we talk about living out our last years. It is actually therapeutic, meaning we all know that this is a shared theme and the possible ways this will unfold, and it helps so much to share our concerns and fears.

So then, let me encourage you, reader: get out a notebook and make your list. Your phone calling could become the highlight of your life.

12:
What about Our Past Sins?

An interesting phenomenon often rears up its head as we age, and it is happening to me right now. I will lapse into a kind of melancholy as I recall some of my more terrible sins, especially those that impacted family members—a wife, a son, a daughter, even a parent or grandparent—and also close friends.

Another way to put it is, as we age we can expect to be reminded of our imperfect human nature and the impact of it as life went on. For some of us, this is very painful, even awful.

For thirteen and a half years, out of the Protestant Chapel at San Quentin Prison in Marin County, a 10-minute drive from where I live, I engaged in cell-to-cell ministry along with several other fellow Christians under the leadership of Chaplin Earl Smith. We mostly visited either North Block or West Block cell areas. I went on Thursday evenings after count had cleared and then proceeded into one block or another. The most unsettling was visiting West Block, where the newly incarcerated prisoners were housed. Often, I talked with guys who were still in street clothes, meaning they were transported and checked into the prison that day.

The gang members were obvious, as they had been locked up before, and other guys who had been in and out of prison over a large period of their lives adjusted quickly. Others were just glad to be in a place where they could get some help. Some of the new guys who looked more like me to some degree were obviously there for the first time, and in many cases, they were scared to death. As I right this, I can picture a couple of these frightened guys right now crying and crying, begging me to contact their families, wives, kids, etc. I was not permitted to do this, of course, and I don't recall ever doing so. There were strict limits on what outside visitors, even those of us with official group training, could do on behalf of prisoners.

My point being, what sins we have committed in the past can grab hold of us and not let go. If I could make a list of mine that have risen up in my memory right now, it would not be a short one. Some of these sad events will cling to me for the rest of my days, and oddly enough, I have been going through this for a few years now, and it seems to be multiplying.

One of my friends reminded me of this weird phenomenon just last Sunday as we sat outside the church building on the benches on the front porch. He admitted to me (it was just the two of us there) that he was struggling with stupid, dumb, rebellious stuff he had done in his life. Immediately I told him I was, too. This relived both of us right away, since we saw it was not just one or the other of us who felt he was going a bit crazy. Here now is how our conversation continued, shortened some of course:

As born-again followers of Jesus we understand that all our sin was placed upon Jesus as He hung on that cross, and that all my sin, past, present, and future, is all gone. Jesus died in God's time, called *kairos* time, which is one of two words translated as "time" in the New Testament. And it means that all my sin is covered—past, present, and future—though I sin in *chronos* time, which is ongoing chronological time—hour by hour, year by year, decade by decade. Jesus died in chronos time but covered all the believer's sin in kairos time. Don't' fret if this does not make sense to you, but as I have discovered over the years, it will some day.

Though we cannot grasp this completely, there it is. Most of the shame and suffering that comes to me as I recall my really bad sins is ameliorated to a great degree when I grasp this incredible truth.

13:
Show Up Often at Your Local Church

From the beginning, it was intended by Jesus that His followers gather together at least once a week. This history is long and complicated, but it is what Christians habitually do, and for a number of reasons. We pray and worship the Lord, we are taught Scripture, proclaim the core Gospel message, and have fellowship together. Acts 2:42 gives a clear and concise description of what that early church did: "And they devoted themselves to the apostles' teaching and the fellowship, to the breaking of bread and the prayers." My focus right now is on fellowship and breaking of bread.

Fellowship—this is being together with friends, our brothers and sisters in Christ. At our Miller Avenue we do a lot of this. A number of us show up an hour-and-a-half before the main service, some for the choir rehearsing a special song that we will sing to and/or with the congregation, and following this a several of us sit out in the front porch and just talk together. Then following the hour-and-a-half service we have lunch together, and this lasts at least an hour. Not all can always stay for the lunch, but most do, and it is the best time of fellowship. We have been doing this for over thirty-five years now.

We are not alone, we are part of a spiritual family, and we talk and talk together, forming lasting friendships. Indeed, this is so vital as we are growing older.

I am just guessing here, but I think that my wife Katie or I speak on the phone with at least half the congregation every week. And then three days a week I email out chapters of books I have written. (Also, these single chapters go up on my blog and to my Facebook friends.)

If you do not have a local church to attend, and I mean after you have diligently searched for one, join us via Zoom. There is a link on the home page of milleravenuechurch.org. Also, you can ask to be added to our contact list at that site. But it is far better to find a real church, being aware that finding the absolute ideal congregation here on the planet is not the goal. Miller Avenue Church is not perfect. No, that is yet to come in our eternal place of worship.

Last, let me encourage everyone reading this to get involved in some form of ministry at the church you find. Fellowship becomes more alive as we work with others to do some sort of ministry, and you don't have to have a seminary degree to do this. In our little church, at least nine people teach or preach, several setup or fix lunch, several pickup and deliver donated food, run the audio/visual process for services, crew on TV shows, do building repairs, run the Sunday school, do street evangelism, do janitor work, run a Spanish-speaking service, hand out bulletins and help new folks find a seat, keep the lending library in front of the church filled with literature, plant new trees, take fellow congregants to doctor appointments, and many other ways that anyone can get involved, not to mention the official capacities of church officers and council members.

Being involved in a local church brings a much fuller experience of faith community than watching recorded or live-streamed or even interactive online services ever can. However, if you are homebound or live too far from a church to which you can easily travel, the online versions are at least there for you and are definitely better than nothing. We have several people who are regulars with us via the Zoom connection—two housebound and others who live hundreds of miles distant.

I hope you let nothing deter you from your search.

14:
Read, Read, Read

I subscribe to "nerdy" magazines and other good Christian publications.

A New Yorker comes in the mail every week, plus the Atlantic, Christianity Today (CT), and Biblical Archeology arrive regularly. There is also the monthly "Table Talk" from Ligonier Ministries that has a meditation for each day of the month and theological studies at a high level. Everyone in the church gets a free copy.

One of the results of this reading, besides information, is the stimulus for keeping the mind healthy and alert, since all of these publications, though not all from a Christian point of view, will exercise the brain. They are not simple reads, but I love them, because I have to really focus to understand much of it. Not all the pieces in these publications are of interest to me, but I really have to dig in. It's good for me.

In addition, I try reading books about topics I enjoy, one at a time, often focusing on a historical theme. I also subscribe to two local newspapers. All of this I recommend to anyone like me who needs to exercise the brain toward the later years.

15:
See Your Doctor and Take Your Meds

Besides my daily vitamin pill, I take three other prescribed medications for one thing or another. I've been doing this for a few decades now. Recently, however, I have been diagnosed as finally crossing the line from pre-diabetic to actual type 2 diabetic. I can't say that I feel any different, but numbers are numbers.

I was a medic in the Air Force for four years—1961–1965—and I learned the value of taking good care of myself, so for the last forty-three years, I go regularly to the gym, as mentioned in the chapter, "Keep Moving," but my doctor does not let me get away with not showing up at least once or twice a year.

Though I really don't relish medical appointments, I go anyway. Just thinking about having blood drawn or injections for one thing or another raises my anxiety level, and there is a reason for it. When I was going through the medical training at Lackland Air Force Base, about 300 of us took the med course, and my assigned partner was a real jerk. During practice on how to give injections, draw blood and so on, he would intentionally cause me pain. He was a lot bigger than I was, so I was limited in how to respond! I admit, I am still impacted by that experience and thus have to force myself into making an appointment.

Besides taking care of ourselves, we do it for others, meaning our family and friends. And because we do this, it encourages others to do the same.

We cannot stop the clock—it goes on ticking; but for ourselves, our ministries and outreaches, we want our slowing down and even our endings to impact those we love as little as possible.

16:
Follow Sports Teams

We are big San Francisco 49ers football fans as well as San Francisco Giants baseball fans.

For many years, I was a sports player, and when unable to play, a sports coach, and when even that is in the rear-view mirror, a sports fan. Baseball and boxing were my main activities as a kid, followed later by basketball, baseball, and golf while in high school and my first two years of college. My dad built a boxing ring for my brothers and I in our back yard in Portland, Oregon, and we boxed and boxed for many years. Still to this day, on Fridays at the gym, I do the speed bag and body bag, which does not help my arthritis, but I refuse to give it up.

For eighteen years I coached the baseball team at San Quentin Prison, the San Quentin Giants. (The SF Giants gave us uniforms and equipment.) We published a book on the 2010 Season at San Quentin, titled *Strike Three, You're Out*.

Then for the last twenty years, overlapping some with the prison baseball, I coached high school baseball at three different high schools here in Marin—sometimes freshman, junior varsity, or varsity teams. This year is the first time in a long time I am not coaching baseball, but I will be back coaching with the junior varsity football team at Terra Linda High School, an eight-minute drive from home. They use me for a variety of tasks but call me "the encouragement coach."

Our television is usually set to record all the games of the Niners and Giants, and we watch most of them. Love it. Actually, it is a must, since at the gym these sports are constantly being discussed, so I have to be up to speed!

Since these sports programs go on most of the year, it prevents me from lapsing into depression. I mean it—we keep ourselves alive by being interested in the trends and the events going on around us, and I do not mean political stuff, which I leave alone.

By the way, Katie says that following and even attending ballet, symphony, and theatrical events is a good substitute for those of us who aren't so sports-minded!

17:
Last Days on the Planet

There is another way to look at the phrase, "on the planet."

It is not such a bad thing, really, to realize that there is a limit to our living. The old proverb "three score and ten and if by reason of strength four score," means living seventy or even eighty years and captures the fact that we are going to die at some point, even if one could last to be two hundred.

I'm eighty-two years old, rickety already, and it keeps on creeping up, and I can see that at some point I will be looking forward to dying, peacefully I hope; but there will be an end of me.

The planet isn't doing so well either, and science tells us that our whole universe will one day be gone, either burn up or freeze out—plus one or minus one is a way of putting it. But here we are on the planet, living our lives out as best we can, knowing full well that our last days on the planet are coming.

18:
Look to Jesus

Even the most content and secure followers of Jesus will be impacted by the reality that they will die, unless Jesus returns before that. Even if one felt certain that this would happen before their death, it is still not enough to suppress all anxiety and fear; these just go with being human.

Over the course of my life, I've had no doubt of the truth of the Bible, our Christianity, nor my personal salvation. For one thing, I was suddenly converted just moments prior to my baptism, and that was when I was twenty-one years old. Then during my ministry, the healings (of myself twice), the almost countless numbers of times when demons were cast out—real stuff, not funny business—and my absorbing the incredibleness of the Scripture, and seeing people's lives radially impacted. I could fill other books on it, more than I already have.

Yes, as the song goes, "Turn your eyes upon Jesus."

Other Titles

The following are books written by Kent Philpott with help from Katie Philpott (in reverse order of publication date) Most are available in both paperback and Kindle versions:

Why I Decided Not to Kill Myself (10/2023)

Pathways to Darkness; Exposing the Dangers of Contemporary Spiritualities (9/2023)

For Those Who Have Made Shipwreck of their Faith (4/2023)

Who Is Muhammad's Gabriel? (1/2022)

A Marriage Manual for Former Homosexuals (11/2021)

Strike Three, You're Out!: Baseball at San Quentin: The 2010 Season (11/2021)

Líbranos del Mal: Cómo Jesús Echa Fuera Demonios Hoy (Spanish Edition) (6/2021)

A Manual of Demonology and the Ocult (4/2021)

Deliverance Handbook: A Guide to Casting Out Demons for Today's Christian (2/2021)

In the Wrong Body?: Transgender Issues from a Biblical Perspective (11/2020)

Other Titles

Dangerous Worship: Book #5 in the Little Book Series (6/2020)

T*he Third Sex? Revisited: Homosexual and Transgender Issues from a Biblical Perspective* (2/2020)

Islamic Studies, 2nd Ed.: Equipping the Christian Witness to Muslims (8/2019)

What's So Bad about Hell?: Book #4 in the Little Book Series (1/2019)

Spiritual Health: Book #3 in the Little Book Series (11/2018)

Biblical Christianity is Evangelical: Book #1 in the Little Book Series (6/2018)

If Allah Wills (English Edition) (4/2016, 2018)

If Allah Wills (Arabic Edition) (1/2018)

False Prophets Among Us: A Critical Analysis of the New Apostolic Reformation (5/2017)

If God Wills: Bringing the Crescent to the Cross (8/2016)

Memoirs of a Jesus Freak, 2nd ed. (5/2016)

Christian Basics: Lessons, Debates, and Conversations (2/2015)

Deliver Us from Evil: How Jesus Casts Out Demons Today (12/2014)

Are You Really Born Again: Understanding True and False Conversion (1/2005), also released as *A Matter of Life and Death* (8/2014)

Why I Am a Christian - Volume 2 (8/2014)

The Soul Journey: How Shamanism, Santeria, Wicca, and Charisma are Connected (7/2014)

Awakenings in America and the Jesus People Movement (11/2013)

If the Devil Wrote a Bible (6/2013)

How to Care for Your Pastor: A Guide for Small Churches (1/2007)

Are You Being Duped? (7/2004)

Why I Am a Christian (5/2002)

For Pastors of Small Churches (2/2001)

www.ingramcontent.com/pod-product-compliance
Lightning Source LLC
Chambersburg PA
CBHW061806070526
44586CB00023B/2731